BEGINNING BEETHOVEN FOR PIANO

ISBN 978-1-84609-765-2

Boston Music Company

EXCLUSIVELY DISTRIBUTED BY

Visit Hal Leonard Online at
www.halleonard.com

World headquarters, contact:
Hal Leonard
7777 West Bluemound Road
Milwaukee, WI 53213
Email: info@halleonard.com

In Europe, contact:
Hal Leonard Europe Limited
1 Red Place
London, W1K 6PL
Email: info@halleonardeurope.com

In Australia, contact:
Hal Leonard Australia Pty. Ltd.
4 Lentara Court
Cheltenham, Victoria, 3192 Australia
Email: info@halleonard.com.au

Series Editor David Harrison.
Music edited by Rachel Payne.
Cover designed by Michael Bell Design.
Cover picture courtesy of Hulton Archive/Getty Images.
Printed in the EU.

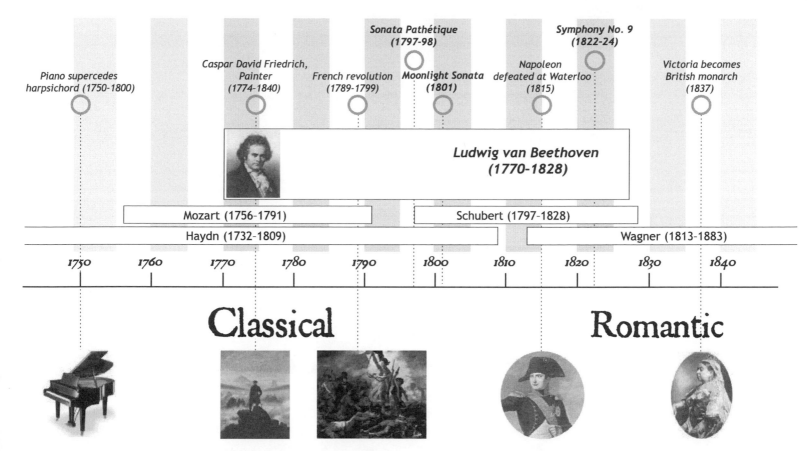

Classical

Romantic

Ludwig van Beethoven was born in Bonn in 1770. By the time of his death in 1827, he was lauded throughout Europe – 10,000 people attended his funeral in Vienna. Beethoven was undoubtedly the dominant composer of the 19th century. His compositional style has influenced almost all composers of western music since in some form or other, and he is counted as one of the most admired composers ever.

Although he was taught piano and violin by his father, Beethoven's first important teacher was Christian Gottlob Neefe, for whom he acted as assistant court organist in Bonn. Beethoven developed a reputation as a fine pianist, and when he was 17, Neefe took his student to Vienna, where he almost certainly met Mozart, and possibly had some lessons with him.

While in Bonn, Beethoven developed a wide circle of friends; his role at the court meant that these included several influential members of the aristocracy. Many of these friendships lasted throughout Beethoven's life, and can be seen reflected in the dedications and titles of his compositions, such as the 'Waldstein' sonata and the 'Razumovsky' quartets.

It was, however, in Vienna, one of the most musically active towns in Europe at the time, that Beethoven was to finally settle. He moved there in 1792 and began lessons with Haydn, with whom he had an often-tempestuous relationship. His friends in Bonn enabled him to make swift contact with aristocratic circles in Vienna, and he embarked on a series of public and private concerts, becoming regarded as one of the top virtuoso piano players in Europe.

Beethoven was not always an easy person to live or work with; he suffered from profound periods of depression and despair when he composed little, yet he could produce torrents of compositions in a small space of time, and he often found the Viennese social life overbearing – he is often described as the embodiment of the romantic spirit. In his first years in Vienna he composed the first of his piano concertos, his first symphony – seen by many as the first 'romantic' piece ever composed – and several string quartets and well-known piano sonatas, such as the 'Pathétique'.

By 1801 the first signs of Beethoven's deafness were beginning to appear. He wrote 'If I had any other profession it would be easier, but in my profession, it is a terrible handicap'. During the next few years he wrote the 'Eroica' Symphony No 3, the title page of which was originally dedicated to Napoleon, but which was torn up by Beethoven in disgust when Napoleon pronounced himself Emperor. His famous symphonies 5 and 6 were premiered at the same concert – with No 6 first – in addition to the fourth piano concerto.

Beethoven started work on his 'choral symphony', No 9, in 1822; the famous melody known to us as 'Ode to Joy' appears in the last movement. Beethoven was completely deaf by the time the work saw its first performance. The audience applauded wildly, but Beethoven, wrapped up in his score, did not notice the applause until someone drew his attention to it.

Beethoven's final years were spent composing almost exclusively for string quartet; these are some of his most admired compositions. His legacy has been immense: for composers, for music historians, for analysts, for listeners. For many he is the epitome of the romantic genius.

Jonathan Wikeley, March 2009

Country Waltz (Ländler)

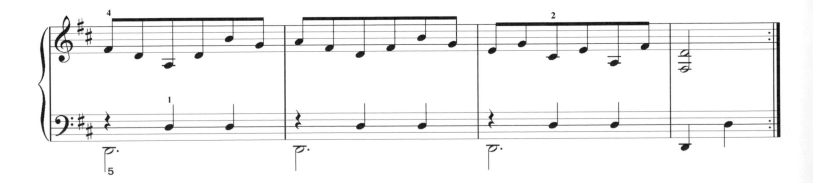

Bagatelle In A Minor

Für Elise (Theme)

Andante con moto

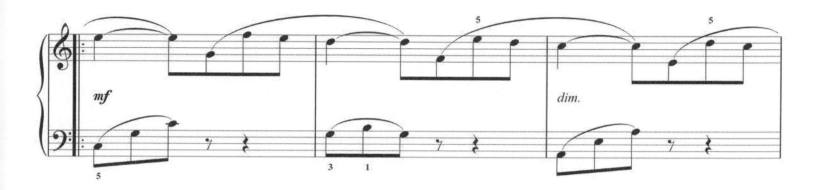

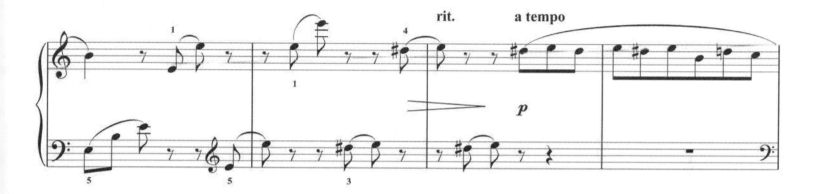

Minuet In G Major

Allegretto

TRIO

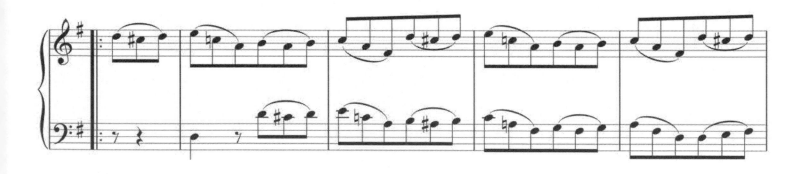

Adagio Sostenuto

Theme from 'Moonlight' Sonata Op. 27, No. 2

Adagio sostenuto

poco rit.   a tempo

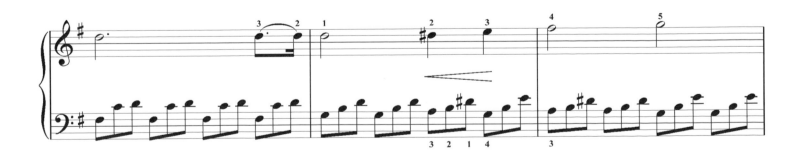

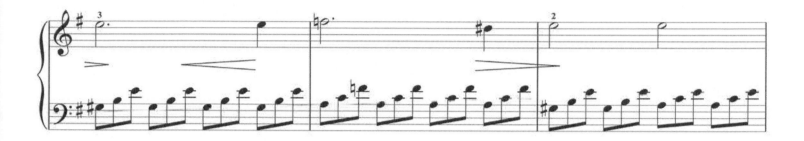

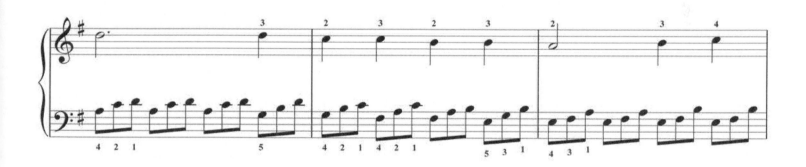

rit.   a tempo

dim.   pp

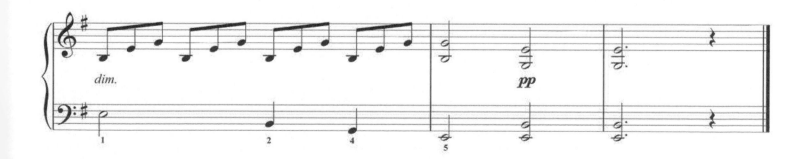

German Dance In G Major

Allegro

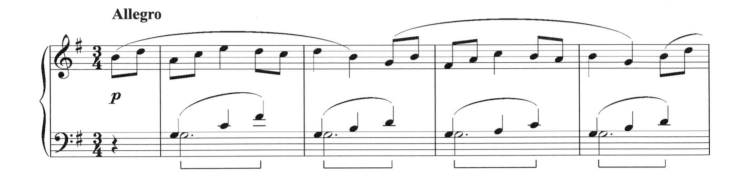

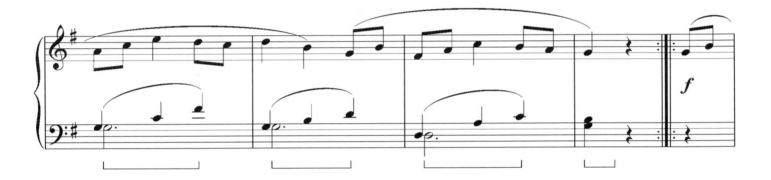

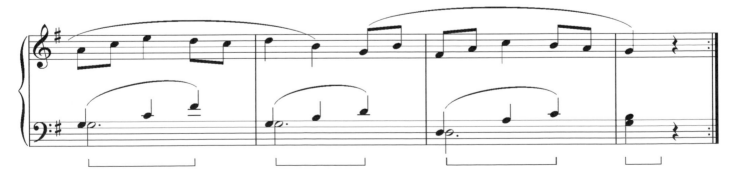

Ecossaise In G Major

Allegretto

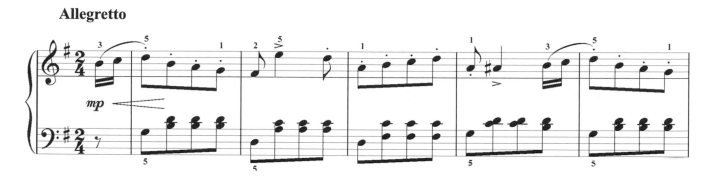

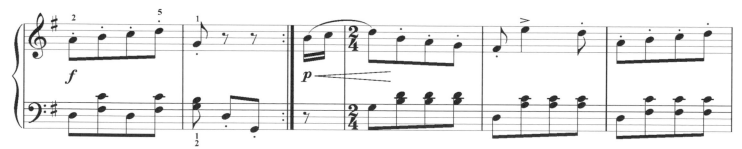

Ode To Joy

Theme from Symphony No. 9, Fourth Movement

Allegro ma non tanto

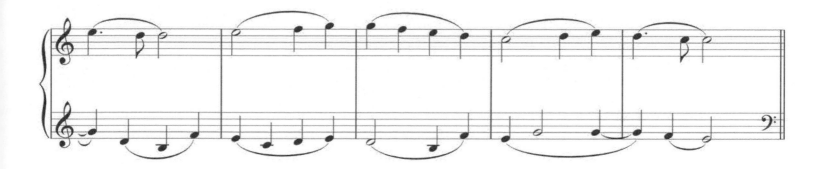

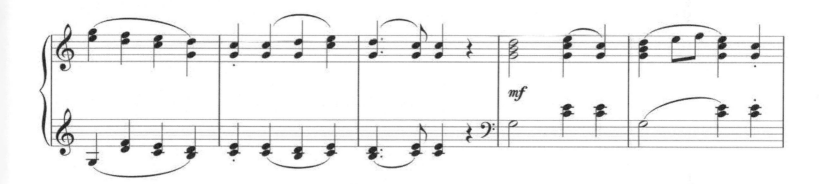

Adagio Cantabile

from Sonata 'Pathétique' Op. 13

Adagio cantabile

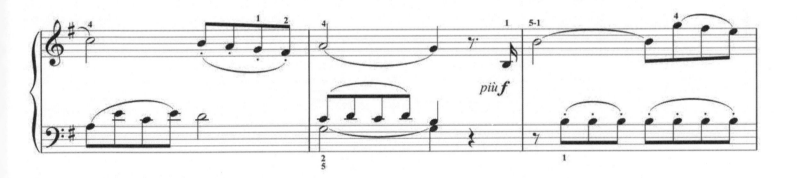

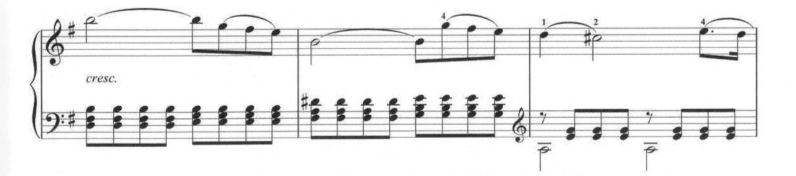

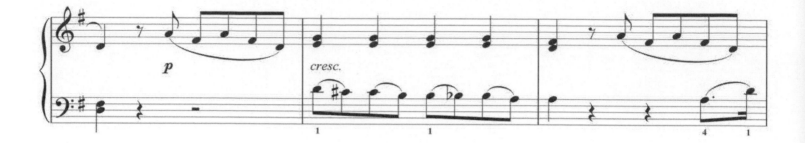

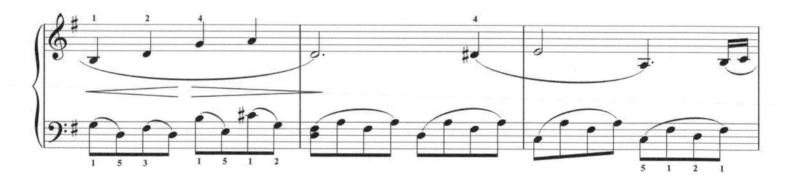

poco rit.

rit.

Ecossaise In E♭ Major

Allegro giocoso

Three Country Dances

I. **Allegro giocoso**

II. **Moderato**

III. Allegro energico

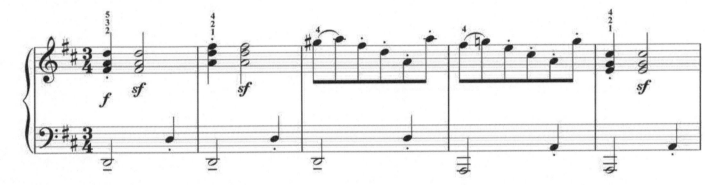

Bagatelle In C Minor

Lento

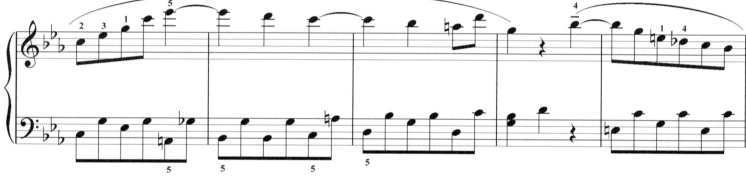

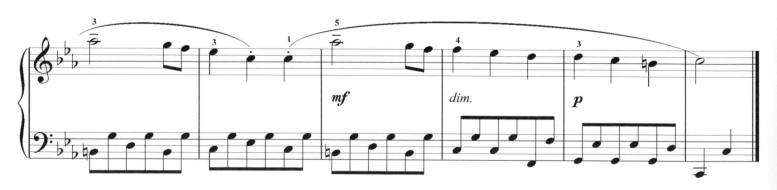

* Originally written in 3/8 time.

First Movement Themes

from Piano Concerto No. 3, Op. 37

Moderately fast

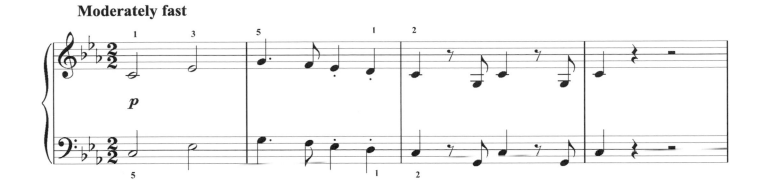

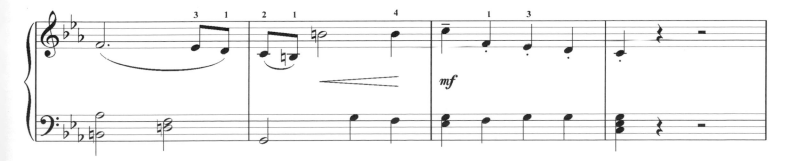

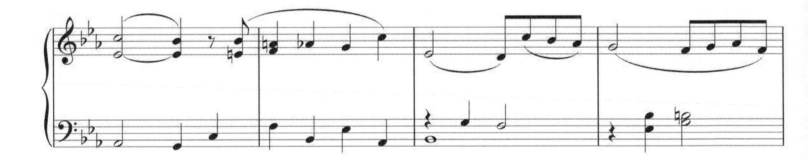

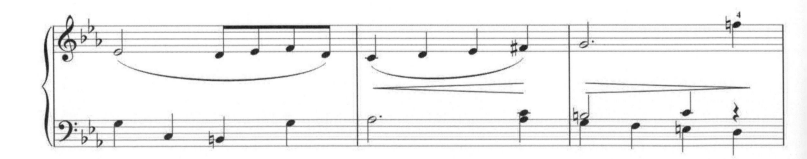

Sonatina In G Major (First Movement)

Moderato

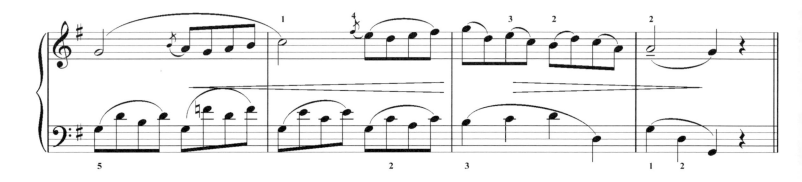

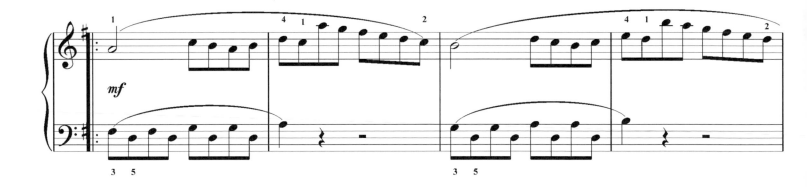

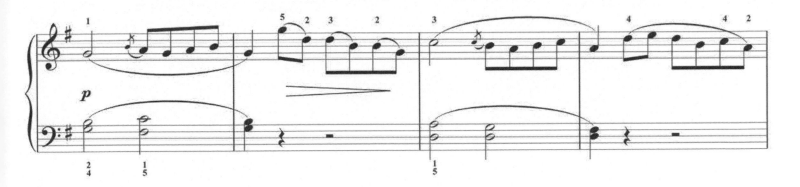

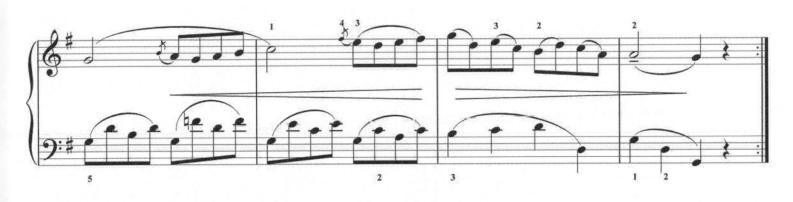

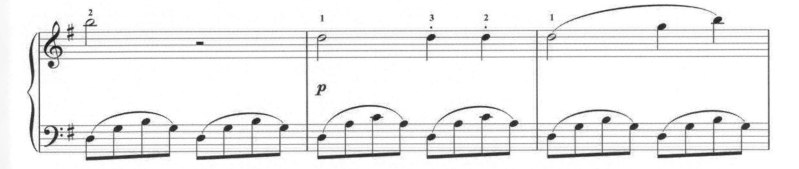

German Dance In D Major

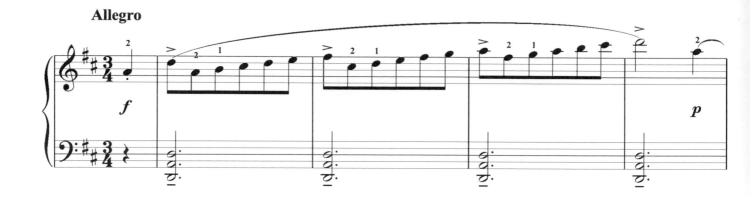

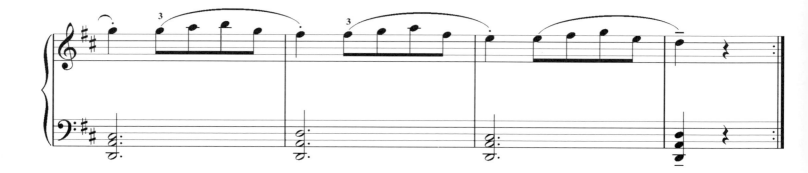

Bagatelle In G Minor

Allegretto

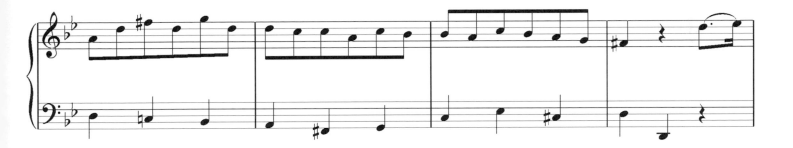

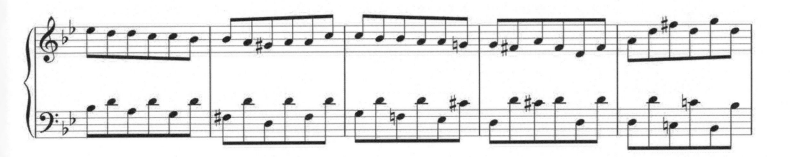

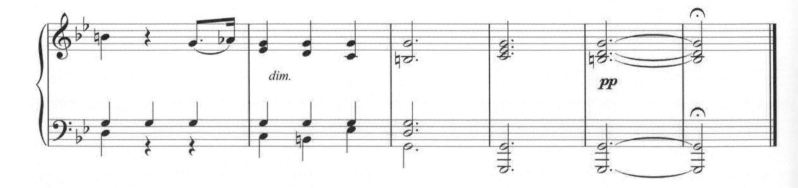